Photosynthesis

Photosynthesis is the way plants make sugar (food) using energy from the sun, water, and carbon that is present in the air in the form of **carbon dioxide** gas.

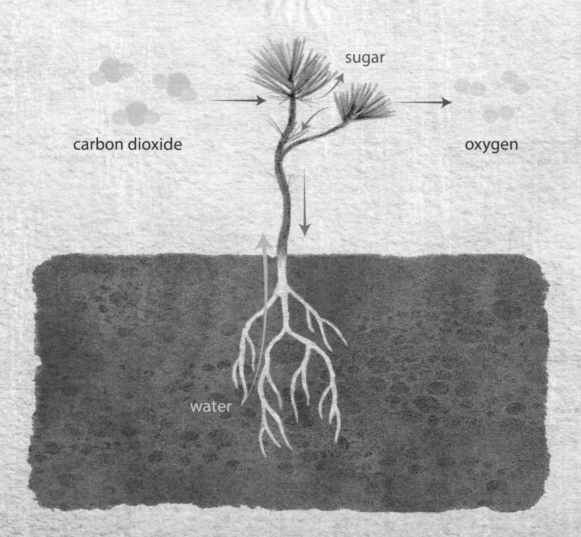

sunlight

sugar

carbon dioxide

oxygen

water

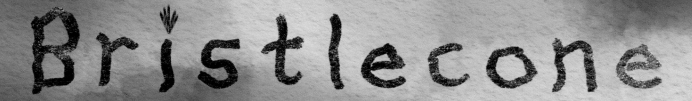

Bristlecone

The Secret Life of the World's Oldest Tree

ALEXANDRA SIY   Illustrated by MARLO GARNSWORTHY

Web of Life
CHILDREN'S BOOKS

CANADA

Washington

Montana

Oregon

Idaho

Wyoming

UNITED STATES OF AMERICA

Nevada

Utah

Colorado

California

Arizona

New Mexico

MEXICO

● The Ancient Bristlecone Pine Forest

● Where Great Basin bristlecone pines live

There are secrets down there.

WHITE MOUNTAINS

*The Ancient Bristlecone
Pine Forest*

See those black specks? They're trees growing on white dirt.

That's unusual. But it's not a secret.

Follow that winding road through sagebrush.

High in the mountains, where the air is thin, a forest grows in gritty **ravines** and on rocky ridges.

That's interesting.
But it isn't a secret.

Watch the summer sun dip behind White Mountain Peak.

Now the air feels cold as the moon rises above a forest of pine trees.
They are the oldest trees on Earth.

That's amazing.
But not a secret.

Night turns to morning, and the rising sun dances with ancient, twisty trees. One of them is named **Methuselah**.

In 1957, scientists determined it was 4,789 years old, making it the oldest known tree on Earth. But now there are rumors of even older trees living close by. One ancient bristlecone pine is thought to be more than 5,000 years old.

Which tree is it?
That's a secret.

The oldest tree in the world is full of secrets.

Its story begins with a seed. Soaked in a pool of melted snow, it swells and opens.

Roots, no thicker than a thread, reach inside a rocky crack.

A skinny stem peeks out at the sun.

Stretching skyward, the stem grows needles. One, two, three, four, five needles in each green bundle.

Living on **snowmelt**, sunshine, and air, the **seedling** grows.

Summers are short, and snow flies each fall, burying the seedling in a cold winter blanket. When spring finally arrives, melted snow drenches its roots and sunshine warms its needles again.

Winter, spring, summer, and fall, Earth moves in a ring around the sun. The seedling makes rings, too. One **growth ring** for each year of its life.

A tree ring has two layers. The light-colored layer grows in the spring. The dark layer forms in late summer.

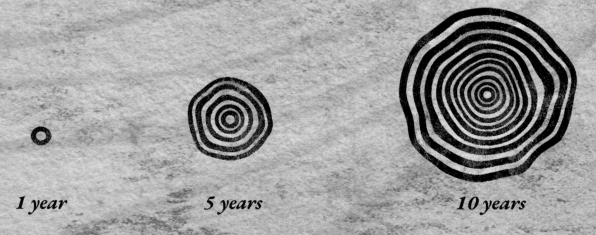

1 year   *5 years*   *10 years*

Bristlecones record environmental conditions in their growth rings.

More moisture makes a wider ring.

Drought slows growth so much that a ring may not form at all.

Extreme cold damages wood as it grows, making a frost ring.

Fire scars form when scorched wood is flooded with sticky **resin**.

Branches flexing, needles sunning, sugar surging, **sap** flowing, roots soaking—
the seedling grows, ring by ring.

30 cm

1 foot

15 cm

6 inches

After fifty years and fifty rings, it is less than six inches tall.

Branches flexing, needles sunning, sugar surging, sap flowing, roots soaking—the **sapling** grows, ring by ring.

After three hundred years and three hundred rings, it is three feet tall.

Winter, spring, summer, and fall, Earth makes rings around the sun. The bristlecone makes rings too. And one spring, it makes something new…

Pinecones!

They pop from thick green branches.

The purple cones are round and plump.
Small red cones are packed with yellow **pollen**.

A few pollen grains stick to a purple cone and sneak inside through tiny holes.

Within a few weeks, the cone grows sharp spikes.

Finally, a bristlecone!

When winter comes, the cone shivers like an ornament on a snow-covered branch. Hidden inside is a secret waiting to form.

Then as spring sunshine melts away the snow, the secret grows into seeds.

Tucked inside each seed is a brand-new baby bristlecone.

On a sunny fall day, the pinecone opens, releasing its seeds. Most of them land in the dirt and are eaten by birds and squirrels.

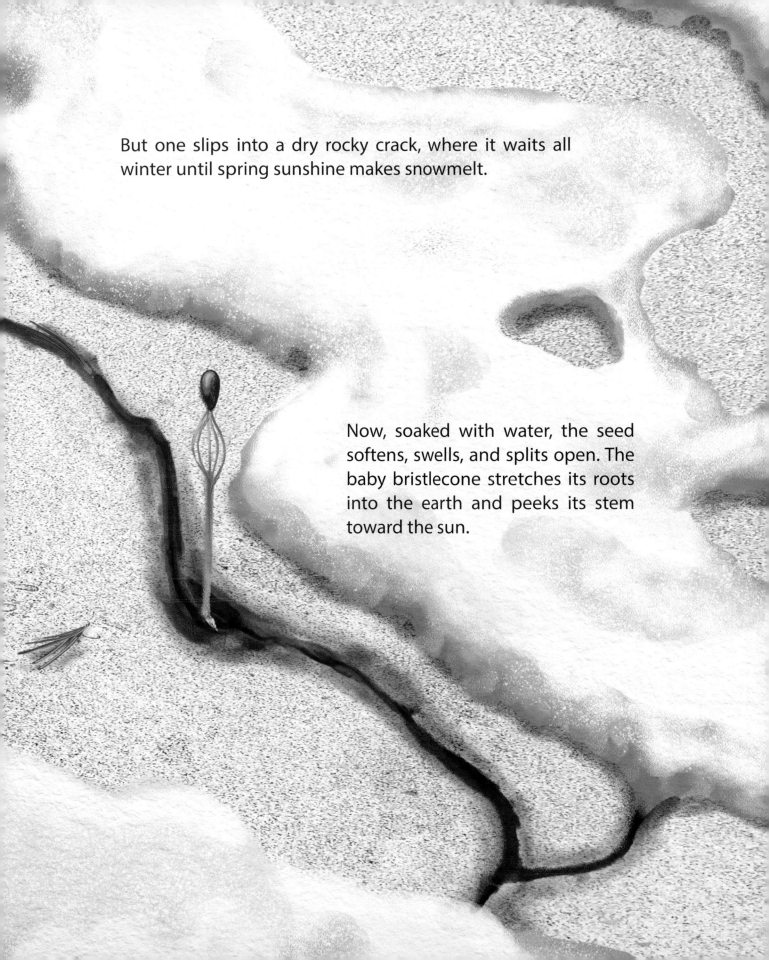

But one slips into a dry rocky crack, where it waits all winter until spring sunshine makes snowmelt.

Now, soaked with water, the seed softens, swells, and splits open. The baby bristlecone stretches its roots into the earth and peeks its stem toward the sun.

Branches flexing, needles sunning, sugar surging, sap flowing, roots soaking—the ancient bristlecone pine grows, ring by ring.

Each summer, sunlight blazes through the thin mountain air, bleaching its bark.

Autumn **squalls** sandblast its old branches, chiseling and sculpting them into twisted shapes.

Winter winds whip icy shards, carving patterns in its trunk.

And one spring day, a **fungus** silently settles down and grows, staining the wood with black designs.

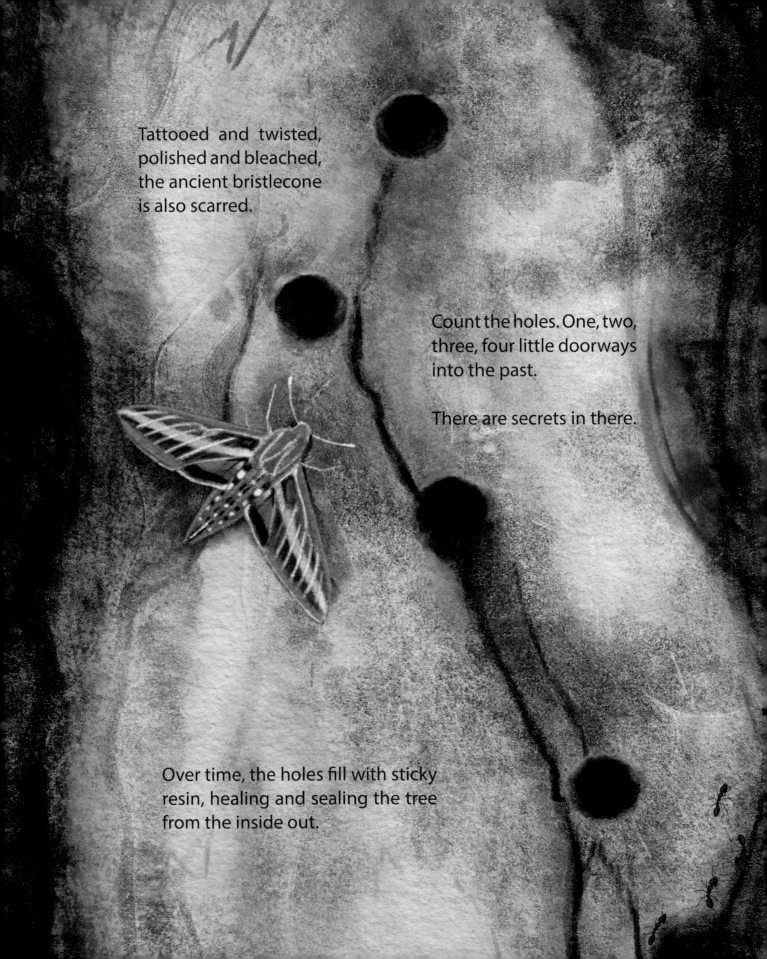

Tattooed and twisted,
polished and bleached,
the ancient bristlecone
is also scarred.

Count the holes. One, two,
three, four little doorways
into the past.

There are secrets in there.

Over time, the holes fill with sticky
resin, healing and sealing the tree
from the inside out.

Those holes were made by scientists with a boring bit, a sharp tool used to drill deep into trees. Its purpose is to pull out long tubes of wood called cores.

The cores have stripes. Each stripe is a tiny part of a growth ring.

Scientists take cores from different places on the tree.

They study the cores, looking for patterns.

40 rings

33 rings

23 rings

17 rings

Then they line up the ring patterns so they match.

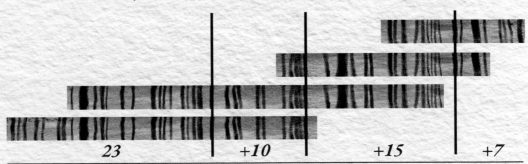

23　　*+10*　　*+15*　　*+7*

55 rings = 55 years

Finally, they count the rings and add them together to find out the tree's age.

The oldest wood is called the **heartwood** because it is in the center of the trunk. It is red and filled with spicy-smelling resin.

For thousands of years, ice and sand have chiseled, scoured, and sculpted some of the younger wood away until the heartwood is on the outside.

A crimson heart is like an ancient symbol that says "forever."

Will the ancient bristlecone pine tree live forever?

Ancient bristlecones don't die from old age. And they aren't easily killed.

Their wood is dense and hard, making them resistant to insects and diseases. They live at high **altitude** where forest fires are rare. They grow slowly in a dry, harsh environment where other kinds of trees could never survive.

Nothing lives forever, not even bristlecone pines.

Long before the ancient bristlecone sprouted and grew its first ring, other bristlecone pines lived and died in valleys of vast forests. It was a colder time when dire wolves and ground sloths roamed the land and enormous birds called incredible teratorns soared overhead.

Slowly, the climate warmed, and animals and plants were forced to **adapt**—or else go **extinct**. Bristlecones adapted by growing higher and higher on mountainsides where it's cold most of the year.

Ancient and strong, the bristlecone is a mystery, living long where life is hard.

And hidden within its rings are thousands of years of stories about

insect attacks,

fires,

heatwaves,

droughts,

floods,

cold snaps,

volcanic eruptions,

and **solar storms** that flared on the surface of the sun.

Rings from both living bristlecones and dead trees paint a picture of Earth's **climate** dating back 10,000 years.

By studying Earth's past, can we glimpse its future?

Branches flexing, needles sunning, sugar surging, sap flowing, roots soaking—the ancient bristlecone pine is still growing, safe and strong in its place in the sun.

It has secrets to share.

Like a history book, the bristlecone is filled with secrets about the past, waiting to be discovered by anyone who can read its rings.

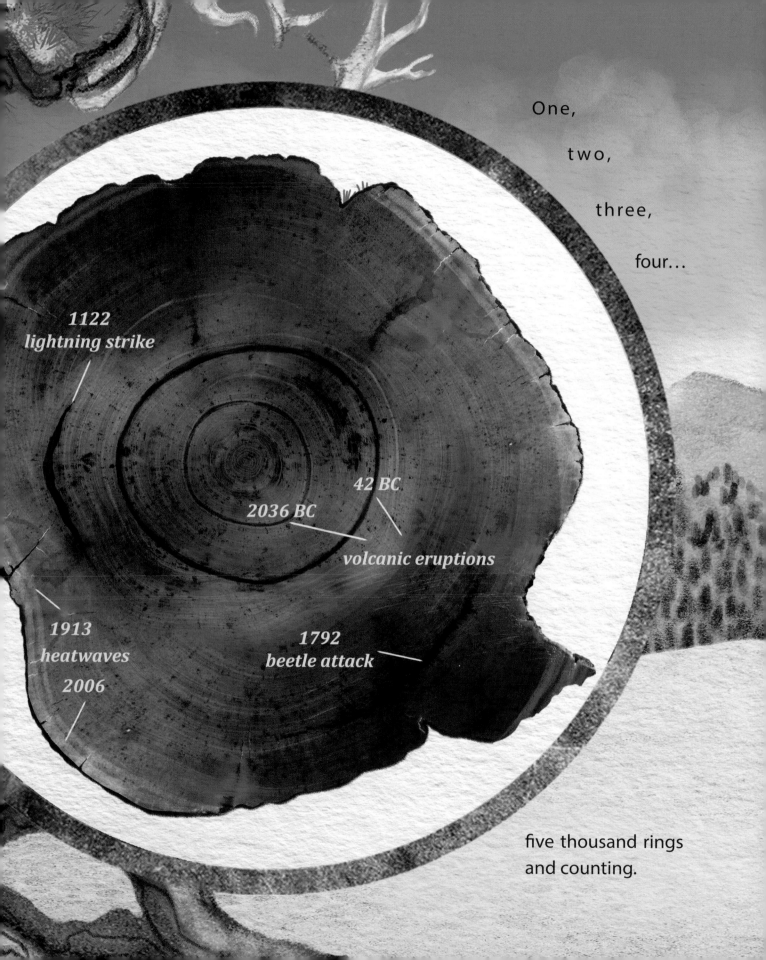

One,

two,

three,

four...

1122
lightning strike

42 BC

2036 BC

volcanic eruptions

1913
heatwaves

1792
beetle attack

2006

five thousand rings
and counting.

MORE ABOUT BRISTLECONE PINE TREES

The Great Basin bristlecone pines in this book grow in the Ancient Bristlecone Pine Forest in the White Mountains, California. To protect the oldest bristlecones, scientists keep their exact locations secret. The Methuselah Tree was the world's oldest known tree for many decades. Recently, scientists have identified older trees; however, they are more interested in how bristlecones are able to live for more than 5,000 years, and in the scientific information contained in tree rings.

Ancient bristlecone pines grow at high elevations (9,000 to 11,600 feet, around 2,700 to 3,500 meters) where harsh conditions inhibit the growth of other kinds of trees. Bristlecones are mostly bare, dead trunks that provide support for the living wood growing beneath narrow strips of bark. Like a lifeline, this thin ribbon of wood carries water to lush branches. Uneven growth and exposure to thousands of years of windblown ice and soil create the bristlecone's twisty trunks and spiral branches.

The soil in the White Mountains lacks many nutrients. The forest receives less than 12 inches (30 centimeters) of moisture a year, which mostly falls as snow. When the snow melts in spring, the forest is soaked with water for a short time. The rest of the year, bristlecones experience drought. Despite the dry environment, forest fires are rare. A lightning strike can set a tree on fire, but fire doesn't spread, because bristlecones grow far apart. A scorched bristlecone floods itself with resin, protecting against rot for centuries. Trees also release resin during insect attacks. Resin contains chemical clues that show scientists whether a wound was caused by fire, insects, or disease.

Severe drought, heartwood rot, or root fungus sometimes kills a bristlecone. But it is the harsh climate and poor soil that slow growth, making bristlecone wood very dense and resistant to disease, fire, and insect damage. Exactly how dense are bristlecones? It can take more than one hundred years for a bristlecone to grow to a thickness of one inch (2.5 centimeters)!

Since bristlecones record environmental conditions in their growth rings, they are important for climate research. Scientists compare bristlecone rings to the rings of ancient deadwood from trees that grew in other parts of the world to help them determine how the climate has changed over thousands of years. For example, scientists have linked bristlecone "frost rings" — dead wood caused by extended cold temperatures during the growing season — with ancient volcanic eruptions in faraway places. In the years 2036 BC and 43 BC, volcanoes spewed huge amounts of ash into the atmosphere, blocking sunlight and causing cold temperatures across Earth for many months. The evidence of these volcanic eruptions can be found in bristlecone frost rings.

Ancient bristlecone pines are protected by law and continue to be studied. To learn more about ancient bristlecones, please visit these websites:

Inyo National Forest: www.fs.usda.gov/inyo

Great Basin National Park: www.nps.gov/grba/index.htm

Laboratory of Tree-Ring Research: ltrr.arizona.edu

White Mountain Research Center: www.ioes.ucla.edu/wmrc

More stories, photos, and science about bristlecones: www.bristleconebook.com

GLOSSARY

adapt – the ability of living things to adjust to changing conditions in order to survive

altitude – how high something rises above the surface of the Earth at sea level

carbon dioxide – a colorless, odorless gas present in the air; it is produced when fossil fuels, wood, and other carbon-based materials are burned; it is released by living things during breathing and decay and is absorbed by plants in photosynthesis

climate – long-term average of weather patterns (such as temperature, humidity, and rainfall) over seasons, years, or decades, affecting a large region or the entire Earth

drought – long, dry period of time in an area during which there is little or no rain or other moisture

embryo – the embryo is the first leaves, roots, and stem of a plant inside the seed

extinct – no longer existing, as when a group (species) of living things dies out so that there are no more members of the group left on Earth

fungus – a kind of living thing that is neither a plant nor an animal and gets its food by absorbing nutrients from its surroundings; examples are mushrooms, yeasts, and molds

growth ring – a layer of wood that grows during a period of time, usually over one year

heartwood – the center of the tree that gives it strength and keeps it standing

Methuselah – the name given to the oldest bristlecone pine discovered in 1957 (named after the oldest person mentioned in the Bible)

ovule – the female part of a plant that develops into a seed after fertilization (when a male and a female cell unite)

pollen – yellow powder made by male pinecones containing the cells that combine with ovules to make seeds

ravines – deep, narrow valleys with steep sides

resin – clear, sticky material made by plants in response to injury and used for protection against disease and insects

seedling – a very young plant that grew out of a seed

sap – juice that flows inside of trees that contains sugar and minerals needed for growth

sapling – a young tree with a slender trunk

snowmelt – water from melting snow that flows over the surface of the ground

solar storms – large explosions on the surface of the sun that can disrupt power grids on Earth and damage satellites; the chemical evidence of past solar storms is preserved in tree rings

squalls – sudden and violent windstorms lasting several minutes that often bring heavy rain, snow, ice, or sleet

To Sally Kilgallon, my dear aunt, who tells a great story and can keep a secret. ~A.S.

For my dad, ever the aventurous, intrepid traveler, with whom I first saw the exquisite trees called bristlecone pines. ~M.G.

Thanks to Dr. Matthew Salzer of the Laboratory of Tree-Ring Research at the University of Arizona for sharing scientific information about bristlecones and for taking the time to critique the manuscript, and to the Society of Children's Book Writers and Illustrators for awarding me a Nonfiction Work-in-Progress grant, which provided generous financial support for my research. ~A.S.

Thanks to Scott Rasmussen for stellar GIS skills, patience, and making me take kayak breaks, and my amazing mum Patricia Tremayne for her keen artistic eye, blue skies, and eternally cheering me on. ~M.G.

Thanks to our teacher readers Cindy Pfost and Karin Morris for their expertise and keen insights.

For ages 5-9

Published in the United States in 2022 by Web of Life Children's Books, Berkeley, California.

Library of Congress Control Number: 2021939593
ISBN: 978-1-970039-03-0

The art in this book was created using watercolor, sand textures, and digital oil paint.

Book design by Marlo Garnsworthy, Icebird Studio, www.IcebirdStudio.com

Printed in China by Toppan Leefung Printing
Production Date: September 2021
Batch: First

For free, downloadable activities, and for more information about our books and the authors and artists who created them, visit our website: www.weboflifebooks.com

Distributed by Publishers Group West/An Ingram Brand
(800)788-3123
www.pgw.com

Some Animals of the
Ancient Bristlecone Pine Forest
— A field guide to the animals in this book

white-lined sphinx moth

western fence lizard

golden eagle

common raven

red-tailed hawk

Clark's nutcracker

mountain bluebird

northern flicker

Cassin's finch

mountain chickadee

violet-green swallow